Around the Churches
of
EAST DEVON

Walter Jacobson

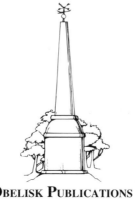

OBELISK PUBLICATIONS

For Audreigh

Acknowledgements
All photographs supplied by Walter Jacobson and Chips Barber
Thanks to the Devon Historic Churches Trust, the *Express & Echo*, and Gemini AM.

First published in 1997 by
Obelisk Publications, 2 Church Hill, Pinhoe, Exeter, Devon
Designed by Chips and Sally Barber
Typeset by Sally Barber
Printed in Great Britain by
The Devonshire Press Ltd, Torquay, Devon

CONTENTS

                                                                         Page

Introduction 4
St Margaret's Church, Topsham 5
Church of the Holy Cross, Topsham 5
Topsham Methodist Church 7
The Parish Church of Clyst St George 7
Clyst St Mary Church 9
St Petrock and St Barnabas, Farringdon 10
St Mary's, Aylesbeare 11
Poltimore Church 12
Broadclyst Parish Church 12
Holy Trinity, Woodbury Salterton 13
St Swithun's, Woodbury 14
Church of the Nativity of the Blessed Virgin, Lympstone 15
Point-in-View Church, Exmouth 16
Holy Trinity Church, Exmouth 17
St John-in-the-Wilderness Church, Withycombe Raleigh 17
Littleham 18
St Peter's, Budleigh Salterton 19
All Saints, East Budleigh 20
St Mary's, Bicton 21
St Michael, Otterton 22
St John the Baptist Church, Colaton Raleigh 23
St Gregory's Church, Harpford 23
Ottery St Mary Church 24
Ottery St Mary United Reformed Church 25
St Andrew's, Feniton 26
St Mary's Church, Whimple 27
St Giles, Sidbury 28
St Giles and St Nicholas, Sidmouth 29
St Peter and St Mary Church, Salcombe Regis 30
St Winifred's, Branscombe 30
Colyton 31

INTRODUCTION

THE following series of articles on Devon churches was written for the *Express and Echo*, starting in 1993 at the request of the Devon Historic Churches Trust. The sources are numerous, including local histories compiled by people who have studied parish records in detail. Beatrix Cresswell's notes on most of the parishes (kept in the Devon Studies Library and based on the works of earlier historians such as Risdon, Westcote, Prince, and Polwhele) were a store of information. Standard reference works were Hoskins' and Mee's books on Devon, and the *History of the Diocese of Exeter* by Boggis. Baring Gould's books added colour to the scene. Other volumes consulted included *Unity and Variety* (a history of the Church in Devon and Cornwall) edited by Nicholas Orme, Chugg's *Devon, The Sacred Yew* by Anton Chetan and Diana Brueton, Crossing's *Guide to Dartmoor*, J.M. Slader's *Churches of Devon*, and P. Underwood's *Ghosts of Devon*.

The purpose of the articles was to create public interest by giving an overall glimpse of parish life down the centuries centred upon churches as the local shrines. People therefore feature rather than detailed study of architecture or ornaments.

Many have shown interest in the series, which was one reason for continuing to write the articles week by week, with the full backing of successive editors of the *Express and Echo*, allowing a small spiritual foothold in a mainly secular medium.

The full text has been stored at the Diocesan Registry at the request of Mr A. M. Barr.

The Church of St Mary, Ottery St Mary

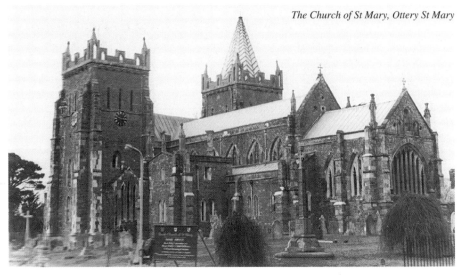

Around the Churches of East Devon

ST MARGARET'S CHURCH, TOPSHAM

ARTISTS and writers agree that one of Devon's finest views is from the churchyard of St Margaret's Church, Topsham, where birds fly over as an ever-widening River Exe goes to meet the sea, with Haldon Hills rising steeply in the background.

The port of Topsham is thought to have operated for at least 2,000 years, through ancient British, Roman, Saxon, and Norman times, and there has been a centre of worship here for at least 1,000 years, perhaps longer, the church being men-tioned in the Domesday Book.

There is an earlier record that King Athelstan in 937 gave Topsham as an endowment to St Peter's Monastery, Exeter.

Although this was confirmed in a document of Leofric, first Bishop of Exeter, it appears King Harold seized the rights and incomes and these fell into the lap of William I. The patronage remained in Royal hands until Henry III handed over to the Earls of Devon.

The churches on the site have all been dedicated to St Margaret, whose symbol, the dragon, is carved on the Norman font, the oldest item in the building. An obscure legend claimed the saint was swallowed by Satan posing as a dragon.

The beast on the font has an object in its mouth, variously conjectured to be Eve's apple, or a fragment from St Margaret's dress. Henry III gave licence for a three-day town fair around July 20, the saint's feast day.

Another early record is the will of Rosemunda Kymmyng, who in 1295 left 4d to the parish chaplain to remember her soul in prayers and 2d to the parish clerk.

Among items listed at a bishop's visit in 1330 were three bells – one to be rung when the priest was taking communion to the sick, the others at funeral processions, asking bystanders to pray for the dead.

Memorials reflect sea connections, including one to Thomas Rundle, quartermaster on HMS *Victory* at Trafalgar.

The brass eagle lectern is in memory of a ship's commander, Richard Pennell, who died in 1797. Master mariner George Hodder, who died in 1700, gave the Dutch chandelier.

The most famous British sculptor of his day, Sir Francis Chantrey, carved the splendid action scene of Admiral Sir John Duckworth, who captured Minorca in 1798, and his son, Colonel Duckworth, who died leading the charge at Albuera (1811).

The Duckworths lived in the property now occupied by the Exeter Golf and Country Club on Topsham Road.

When the church, except for the old tower, had to be rebuilt in 1874, it was Sir J. T. B Duckworth, Bart., whose name appears as laying the corner stone, along with J. A. Leaky (vicar), William Walrond and J. P. Harrison (churchwardens).

The massive new church, with room for 1,000, replaced a building which had not impressed historian Polwhele in 1794: "With additions it is almost square, with a very low roof."

Workmen employed in the rebuilding gave a small lancet window featuring St Margaret.

A famous son of Topsham, Sir William Webb Follet, MP for Exeter and attorney general 1834–44, is also commemorated. A contemporary said of him: "In every qualification in intellect and grace of manner he was as nearly perfect as man can be."

CHURCH OF THE HOLY CROSS, TOPSHAM

THE STORY of Topsham this century has been enriched by the faith and energy of a retired priest, which led to the building of the Roman Catholic Church of the Holy Cross.

Author Arthur Mee in his book, *Devon*, describes how he found Father J. J. Cahill "young at 80 digging in the garden round the church he had built after 40 years missionary work on another continent."

He had in fact spent 40 years in New South Wales and New Zealand, where he was responsible for the building of a fine church in Wellington Province. That experience must have been a help when he set about establishing a new church at Topsham.

An old (Topsham) Wesleyan chapel, which had been taken over for services by the small band

of Catholics, was declared unsuitable by Bishop Barrett (of Plymouth) in 1932, and the congregation of 12 was taken by taxi each Sunday to worship at the Church of the Blessed Sacrament in Heavitree.

Fr Cahill saw an opportunity in 1934 when a property and house on high ground above the railway line became available, personally giving £600 towards the total price of £1,600. When it came to building the new church on the site, £500 more was required before the bishop would agree to the work going ahead.

Could Fr Cahill spare the £500 out of money he had saved against the needs of his old age? He decided he could.

The bishop replied: "If you do that you may go ahead." Next day (church records report) Fr Cahill signed the contract with Turl Bros – "two promising young builders of Topsham, for £1,350, and they did a fine job of work."

The church was dedicated by Bishop Barrett on the Feast of the Exaltation of the Holy Cross, 14 September 1937.

Sharing the same trade as Jesus the carpenter, builders always regard any church work they do as a special honour. Mr Peter Turl, of Topsham, recalls the pride his late father, Mr Frank Turl, took in the part he had played as an apprentice helping his uncles build Holy Cross Church.

Fr Hugh McKenna, parish priest for many years, told me that the subsequent addition of an entrance porch had cost as much as the original church.

The pre-war congregation of 12 has now grown to 150 worshippers, who come from the East Devon area between Exmouth and Exeter.

Lay ministers lend a hand, including two appointed to administer the chalice at Holy Communion, now that the people receive "in both kinds" (wine as well as bread).

Over the years two women members have received high honours. Mrs Kathleen Pym has the Plymouth Diocesan Award for many years of faithful service. The late Miss Patricia McKenna, of Clyst St Mary, was given the Pope's Bene Merenti Award for her work at the former Marist School in Winslade House, now the London and Manchester Assurance Company's HQ.

A statue of Christ holding a child by the Devon sculptor, Harry Hems, once awarded a gold medal at a Philadelphia exhibition, was bought for a few pounds at an auction by a woman member and installed in the church.

TOPSHAM METHODIST CHURCH

KNOWN with good reason as The Church of Seagoing Men, St Nicholas, Topsham, was built in 1867 after 60 years of Wesleyan (Methodist) activity in the town.

Although it is unusual for Methodist churches to be dedicated to saints, St Nicholas, Bishop of Myra, on what is now the Turkish coast, was a suitable choice. He has been a patron saint of seafarers since reported miraculous rescues of Mediterranean sailors in the 4th century.

Capt John Bagwell Holman emerged as a leading figure, in both the Methodist community and the town, in the early 1800s, when Topsham was an important trading port for ocean-going vessels and also had a large fishing fleet.

Born into a family of seamen – his father died when his ship capsized under Old London Bridge – John became a ship owner, built the town's only dry dock, and pioneered marine insurance in the ports of Topsham and Exeter.

Many members of the Holman family were lost at sea over the years, and whenever John returned from his voyages, his mother always gave "public thanks" for his safe return in the old Friends Meeting House, where the Wesleyans had held services since 1811.

Under the more familiar title of Santa Claus, St Nicholas was also the patron of children, and the church has given youth work priority since the Sunday School was founded in 1820.

The first resident minister, a Mr Sanders, was appointed in the same year.

The congregation realised a long ambition when the new church was opened in 1867. Capt Holman had died four years previously, but the family and fellow seamen feature in the stained glass windows.

The captain's seafaring sons assumed his mantle as church leaders, and with their mother contributed more than £1,000 towards the building in the heart of the town. St Nicholas was designed in the Early English style, with a wooden roof made to resemble the hull of a boat.

Over the years a red-letter day was the annual salmon supper, for which local fishermen provided from their catches in the Exe. This was sadly discontinued when the salmon stocks were depleted.

Band of Hope meetings were enjoyed by children, who paid one old penny for magic-lantern displays with such titles as "The Giant Intemperance and How to Fight Him."

Rugby football was the sport of a young Topsham minister earlier this century. The Rev Kenneth Waights often limped to the pulpit on a Sunday after a torrid game on Saturday, but this did not prevent him from becoming national President of the Methodist Conference in 1971.

Moving with the times, the Rev Robert Blackhall and his congregation rearranged the church plan.

The church hall was sold, and the church interior was altered to include a new hall, kitchen, toilets, Sunday School rooms, and an upstairs lounge. Pews were replaced by movable, comfortable chairs, while the attractive exterior was preserved.

A congregation of 350 was present for the re-dedication on 22 March 1992 by the Rev Kenneth Hext, chairman of the Plymouth and Exeter District. Opportunity was also taken to give thanks for the 125th anniversary of the church.

THE PARISH CHURCH OF CLYST ST GEORGE

THIS IS a church that I know well. Rural peace has returned to Clyst St George since the village was bypassed, but motorists who keep within the speed limit on the short length of dual carriageway on the route between Exeter and Exmouth see over on the left a medieval tower with a clock face. That tower is all that remains of the old building, which was the first English church destroyed by enemy bombs in the Second World War.

In fact, air raid wardens were stationed on the tower during the raid when the incendiaries fell, and a specimen of the bomb may be seen in the porch of the church, which was restored in 1952.

Clyst St George was an early centre for English worship, but there is no trace of the Saxon church, although the local manor was recorded in the Domesday Book.

One of the keenest supporters of Clyst St George Church in recent times was the late Prof Freddie Brimblecombe, whose research into cures for children's diseases earned him world renown. To commemorate the 100th anniversary of the death of the Rev H. T. Ellacombe in 1985, Dr Brimblecombe and his wife Esther wrote a delightful short history of the church, largely from records kept by Miss Betty Gibbs – a descendant of one of the parish's oldest families, the Gibbs of Pytte House.

Another descendant of the Gibbs family, Baron Wraxall, is patron of the church living.

The Rev Thomas Ellacombe's talents and eccentricity made him nationally famous while he was Rector from 1850 to 1885. Does his ghost still stalk the building and ground? One Topsham resident I visited some years ago said that, as a choirboy early in this century, he saw the ghost in the church.

During the Ellacombe festival some years ago a bearded replica of the famous 19th-century Rector, created by some Exeter artists, turned many a startled head in its direction as it stood amid a bower of flower arrangements in the sanctuary.

An engineer apprenticed to the Brunels, Mr Ellacombe is said to have taken Holy Orders after a difference of opinion with his employer, Marc (father of Isambard Kingdom Brunel).

Whatever the reason, he used his skills in rebuilding both church and church school and in inventing a new system of bellringing. So the story goes…

Hearing erratic noises from the bell tower one evening, Mr Ellacombe rushed over from the Rectory to find the bellringers the worse for a potent local cider. He dismissed the lot and set about installing the celebrated Ellacombe chiming system, which could be operated by one person.

Thereafter he was able to summon the flock to worship by himself.

Near at hand the much-loved Lady Seward Church Primary School is still thriving after nearly 300 years. It was founded by Lady Hannah Seward in 1704, in accordance with the will of her husband, Sir Edward Seward of Clyst Court, a famous Devonian of his time.

The school was founded "to instruct the children of Clyst St George in the principles of the holy Christian faith and religion and to teach them reading, arithmetic, and navigation."

The old village stocks can be seen on the north side of the bell tower. In spite of recent reactionary comments in press and radio about how to deal with delinquents, the churchwardens, Maj Harry Robinson and Mrs Ethel Cann, have no immediate plans to bring them back into use!

Dominating the churchyard is the now huge Wellingtonia pine planted in 1868 by Charles Thomas Longley, the Archbishop of Canterbury who called the first Lambeth Conference. He was a friend of Thomas Ellacombe.

The Old Rectory, sold for apartments some years ago, in Thomas Ellacombe's time had a garden of 3,000 different plants – all of which he knew by their Latin names.

CLYST ST MARY CHURCH

FLASHPOINT for the Prayer Book Rebellion of 1549, Clyst St Mary Church was first built in medieval times alongside the Winslade Manor.

Walter Raleigh, father of the great Sir Walter, of East Budleigh, was riding towards Exeter on a holiday when he overtook an old woman going to the church, a half-mile from the village, clutching her rosary and her old Latin prayer book.

Raleigh lectured her. Did she not know that by King's decree on 9 June 1549 (Whitsunday), only the new English Prayer Book was to be used, and all Catholic symbols were forbidden?

The woman ran off and told the loyal Catholic congregation, who swarmed off "like wasps" and barricaded the village against attack. Finding refuge in a chapel for old priests in the village, Raleigh was saved by Exmouth seafarers, possibly his own employees.

Meanwhile Catholic forces from Cornwall and West Devon were besieging the walls of Exeter. Later Raleigh was captured by rebels and imprisoned with others in the tower of the old St Sidwell's Church, then outside the city walls.

The King's general, Lord Russell (later Earl of Bedford), who had acquired great wealth in the West from the dissolution of the monasteries, including Tavistock, assembled an army at one of the Carew family estates near Honiton.

Russell won battles at Feniton and Aylesbeare Common, and the rebels retreated to Clyst St Mary. At Clyst Bridge, now preserved as the oldest structure of its kind in Devon, many villagers lost their lives in a fierce encounter.

Next day fighting continued on the high ground of Clyst Heath, but the brave villagers and Cornish peasants were no match for Lord Russell's German, Italian, and Spanish mercenaries, who hoped for dispensation from the Pope for killing their fellow Catholics in a horrid bloodbath.

Clyst St Mary's thatched cottages were burned to the ground, and the population cut in half by the slaughter.

It seems the Rev William Gybbe, church rector from 1542 to 1562 and also of Clyst St George from 1554, managed to keep his post amid all the changes of the times.

From Saxon times, a parish church has stood near the manor, some distance from the village, but there was also a chapel in the village built as part of St Gabriel's Hospital, established in 1311 by the Bishop of Exeter for 12 aged and infirm priests, tended by two chaplains.

The bishops themselves often lived at Bishop's Court, a mile north of the village, whose eerie chapel is still intact in the building carefully preserved by Taylor's paint firm.

The oldest part of the parish church is the medieval tower, restored some years ago. Records give interesting glimpses into the lives of two local women who worshipped there.

On 29 March 1383, widow Denise Noel was ordered by Bishop Brantyngham to walk around the church barefoot on three successive Sundays as public penance for an unnamed sin.

And in 1856 Charlotte Tapley was given the unlikely job of sexton (digging graves!) "provided her behaviour be such as to please the parish." She held the job just one year.

The church now has for its neighbour the London and Manchester Assurance headquarters, with the old manor house at its centre.

Like St Paul's, Honiton, St Mary's was adapted in the last century to fit in with the terrain by having its sanctuary in the north, instead of the traditional east.

ST PETROCK AND ST BARNABAS, FARRINGDON

HIDDEN discreetly half a mile from the Exeter–Sidmouth road, St Petrock and St Barnabas Church, Farringdon (a name derived from two Anglo-Saxon names meaning Fern Down) serves a charming unspoilt section of East Devon.

The Norman font, where children from the scattered farms and cottages have been baptised over the centuries, is a visible clue that people have worshipped on the site since William the Conqueror's time, and the dedication to St Petrock, the 6th-century Cornish missionary saint, raises conjecture of an even earlier foundation.

The twinning of Farringdon with the Norman village of Sequeville-en-Besin was believed to have special significance by Canon Howard Senar, author of *Farringdon, a Devon Church and Parish*.

What is now known as Bishop's Court, originally part of Farringdon parish, was given to a Norman family, the Sechvilles (or Secquevilles) by William the Conqueror, who was probably related to them.

The grandfather of Farringdon's first named rector, Robert Giffard, married a Sechville.

"So after 900 years from the impact of William the Conqueror, his Norman successors are welcomed into the parish church and homes of Farringdon," Canon Senar wrote.

When the Secqueville visitors shared a service in the church, Farringdon people were surprised that the tune of their traditional Norman hymn was the same as the Liverpool football anthem, "You'll Never Walk Alone".

Bishop Bronescombe of Exeter bought the Sechvilles' property and built Bishop's Court and its chapel, which still stand on the hill above the Clyst River. When the bishop's chaplain there died, the weather was bad and the bishop tried to have him buried at Sowton churchyard, which was nearer than Farringdon.

The funeral procession was stopped by Mr Fomizon, Sowton landowner, and the chaplain's body thrown into the water, to the bishop's anger. What happened next is uncertain, but an unlikely version claimed that the body was miraculously taken up into Heaven.

The earliest recorded burial at Farringdon itself was in 1614 of John Drake, a member of the seafaring family. It is a reminder that, in spite of the rural setting, the parish shared in Devon's naval heritage.

Items in the 1684 churchwarden's accounts support this: "Gave one shilling to eight castaway seamen, having lost all they had." When the church was rebuilt in 1683 "ye workemen were given beer to the value of one shilling."

Protecting the attractive wooden shingle roof from woodpeckers has proved a problem for churchwardens recently. After finding about 100 holes, they installed bird scarers.

A window in Crealy Barton, one of the parish properties mentioned in the Domesday Book, recalls that it was owned for 535 years by King's College, Cambridge.

ST MARY'S, AYLESBEARE

FERTILE Aylesbeare, situated near the main road between the two Roman camps of Exeter and Dorchester, was already an important rural centre when William I captured Exeter in 1067. That explains why the wide church area of East Devon, including Exmouth, Budleigh, and Ottery St Mary, was given the title of Aylesbeare Rural Deanery, which it still retains.

It is likely that there was a church in Saxon times, but records of a stone Norman building emerged when the nearby Minchin Court Manor was given in 1189 to the Abbess and nuns of Polsloe Priory in Exeter. In return, the nuns were expected to employ a vicar to look after the church and people.

About six nuns lived at Minchin, enjoying the country air, producing food for themselves and their city sisters, and daily attending services led by the vicar at St Mary's Church.

Canon Howard Senar, who held a retirement post at Aylesbeare from 1982, records in his fascinating history of Aylesbeare that the nuns were given stern advice by Bishop Walter Stapeldon, who told them: "Speak as little and as quietly as possible, in Latin not French (their native tongue); and say grace before and after meals."

When Devonian Bishop Walter Bronescombe started making records, the first named Vicar of Aylesbeare (in 1261) was Gregorius, or Gregory.

In 1273 all the priests of Aylesbeare Deanery were ordered by the Archdeacon of Exeter to march in procession, clad in vestments, to Ottery St Mary "to warn malefactors" against armed robbery of the church's offerings.

Newton Poppleford people, at the north end of the parish, used to walk to Aylesbeare for Sunday worship and picnic on the common on their return. Because thieves raided their homes in their absence, however, in 1331 a chapel was built in the hamlet, with a priest to look after it.

In the first year of the Black Death, 1349, Aylesbeare had three vicars in succession, and the Newton Poppleford chaplain also died.

The appointment of Robert Drake as vicar in 1545 shows the parish link with the sea, as well as the wool trade. The names Drake, Raleigh, Gilbert, Hawkins, Frobisher, and Plimsoll all appear in the church registers. Ancient beams surviving in Minchin House and Cottage are thought to have come from old naval vessels.

In Robert Drake's time a great battle was fought on Aylesbeare Common, where Lord Russell's mercenaries overcame the forces of the West rebels opposing the new English Prayer Book. Miles Coverdale, future Bishop of Exeter, was chaplain to the King's army.

The elegant light church is free from a surplus of Victorian glass, but there are two charming memorial windows on the south side. One records the 39 years as vicar of William Henry Carwithin, from 1848 to 1887.

Described by a neighbouring vicar as "very straightforward and dogmatic", he had a sense of humour. At his last service he surprised the congregation with his text : "Forty years long was I grieved with this generation..."

The other window is in memory of Lady Newbolt. A frequent visitor to Aylesbeare was Sir Henry Newbolt, who wrote the lines enshrined at Lord's Cricket Ground: "Play up, play up, and play the game."

The Rev Maurice Key, who followed his father as vicar in 1932, later became a much-loved Bishop of Truro. He retired to Newton Abbot.

POLTIMORE CHURCH

ALONG the ancient avenue lined with lime trees, connecting Poltimore House to the parish church of St Mary, came a procession in all weathers in the early days of this century.

Led by the second Lord Poltimore, the staff of the ancient manor house, whose future is now in the balance, were on their weekly church parade, the women in poke bonnets and the men wearing top hats.

As they entered, the staff went to their allotted places in the nave, and the lord and his family to their own pew, which remains intact to this day, complete with its fireplace, in the south transept.

The Bampfyldes owned Poltimore manor from about 1300 to 1940, and one of their line became the first Baron Poltimore in 1831. As memorials in the church bear witness, for those 600 years members of the family left their mark on Devon and the nation's history.

They replaced the original church with the present building in the 13th and 14th centuries, only the curious Norman font remaining, and a pane of stained glass depicting the head of Christ.

The Bampfyldes were active in public life over the years. John was MP for Devon in 1429, another John the first Tiverton MP in 1615, and Sir Charles Bampfyde was elected MP for Exeter six times from 1774 to 1809.

A "kidnapped" boy heir features in old Devon folklore. At first unaware of his rights, the boy grew up and served as a gamekeeper on the estate of his Yorkshire captor, but he lived to see his son eventually take over the Devon manor.

Sir John Bampfylde supported the Parliamentary party in the Civil War, and Exeter Royalists signed a surrender in Poltimore House on 3 April 1646. His nephew, Sir Coplestone Bampfylde, however, took an active role in restoring Charles II, and was rewarded by being appointed first Sheriff of Devon.

Francis Bampfylde, born at Poltimore House in 1615, became a Nonconformist minister and was imprisoned in Dorchester for eight years. Later, as a Baptist minister in London, he refused to take the oath to James II and died in Newgate prison.

Family poet, John Codrington Bampfylde, was also committed to Newgate prison when he broke windows in Sir Joshua Reynolds' home because the artist refused to let him woo his niece.

It is thought that this poet may have written the inscription on the churchyard tomb of William Fidoe, coachman to Sir Richard Bampfylde, who died aged 42 in 1752.

Coachman! Yet Foe to Drink, of Heart sincere
In manner gentle and in Judgement clear;
Safe thro' ye chekerd Track of Life he drove,
And gained ye Treasure of his master's love.

Local historian Dr Richard Fortescue-Ffoulkes, who ran a nursing home at Poltimore House after the Second World War, draws attention to the curious bench carvings of John Fortescue, rector for 34 years, and his wife, who (unlike her husband) was given a halo by the artist.

The longest-serving rector was in office for 52 years. He was, of course, a Bampfylde.

BROADCLYST PARISH CHURCH

SEEN from the motorway and all the roads for miles around, Broadclyst church tower is the finest in Devon. No less an authority than Preb John Scott, Devon's leading expert on church bells and clocks, offered the people of Broadclyst this personal view in a recent lecture. All who agree with him can take heart that the tower has now been restored at a cost of £116,000, representing great local effort and a gift from English Heritage.

The bells are among the best, too, and were increased from six to eight in 1897 to celebrate Queen Victoria's diamond jubilee.

As at Clyst St George, the gruesome stocks are preserved in the churchyard near the unusual double lychgate, and standing prominently by the path is a splendid medieval preaching cross.

Recent vicars have given a nod to tradition by delivering a sermon there on Palm Sunday before the congregation processes into church through the south porch.

The porch itself was renovated recently – as a memorial to Sir Richard Acland, the 15th baronet, a member of the well-known Devon family whose home has been at Broadclyst since the 16th Century. Sir Richard made the Killerton gardens available to the public through a gift to the National Trust.

A 1614 memorial to John Acland, who moved here from North Devon, is in the north-east corner and in the same area is a beautiful modern stained-glass window in memory of Ellen, daughter of Sir Francis Acland, a child of 11 years killed in a bicycling accident in 1924. Older parishioners remember Ellen.

Nearby a plain wood cross hangs on the wall, given in memory of kindly Wilfred Westall, Devon's well-loved bishop of recent times, who spent his last years in Broadclyst.

As Bishop of Crediton, he became a national figure after the Second World War. An outstanding preacher and public speaker, he was so much in demand from all quarters, that many of us found that we had booked Bishop Wilfrid in vain for what we thought was an important occasion. It would seem that he could find himself unwittingly booked on the same day for, say, a national BBC chat show, a conference in Edinburgh, and a Devon parish event, and at the last moment had to choose where he should be! He replied to letters in immaculate longhand by return of post.

Lady Anne Acland, the author of the acclaimed book, *A Devon Family*, described in a short parish history how a load of rotten timber and carvings was taken from the church interior, including the roof, in 1832.

Sir Thomas Acland asked what was in the cart. "If you please, Sir Thomas, angels," was the reply.

When the roof needed replacing again, at a cost of £80,000, Treasurer for the appeal was Viscount Knutsford, who lives near the church in Broadclyst House, one of the former vicarages.

HOLY TRINITY, WOODBURY SALTERTON

THE FOUNDATION of Woodbury Salterton as a parish in the 1840s and the continuing welfare of both church and church school in recent years are linked to the generosity of two maiden ladies.

First of these was Miss Marianne Pidsley, who lived in the elegant Georgian home, Greendale, a mile from the village. She was a wealthy member of the Pidsley family, who for some centuries had successfully farmed in the area now known as the Sowton Industrial Estate – home of the new

Express and Echo building.

A person of strong religious convictions, Miss Pidsley's first concern was for the 130 children who had to travel the two miles to Woodbury church twice each Sunday, so she set about building a church and school at Woodbury Salterton.

The church was consecrated by Bishop Phillpotts on 4 September 1844, but the building process was not without incident. The owner of Bridge Farm objected because he alleged the chancel was encroaching on his land. Miss Pidsley promptly bought the farm.

When two robins nested in the unfinished church, Mr Stephens, a sculptor, carved the two birds to be seen in bosses in the chancel arch.

Sadly, falling materials killed John Gibbins, aged 12, as he was watching the builders. His grave is in the churchyard, formerly an orchard.

The embroidery on the sanctuary chair was worked by Caroline, wife of John Walling, the school's first master; they were the first couple married in the new church. When Lady Rolle, herself responsible for the building of Bicton Church, saw the work, she said to her brother Lord Clinton: "There Charles, I have seen a great deal of needlework, but never the equal of this."

The front door of the church still has the lock and key Miss Pidsley secured from the old Exeter Prison, which had just been demolished.

The church school was completed in 1847, and the Vicarage, with its new well – used by the villagers for 100 years – in 1851. The total cost of all these projects was £13,000.

Meanwhile Miss Pidsley died suddenly at 42 during a visit to Tintagel in September 1847, and her burial near the lychgate was witnessed with sorrow by the whole parish.

A later occupant of Greendale House, Lady Dunboyne, gave the parish hall, opened by the Bishop of Exeter in 1910.

A great character in early days, John Skinner, sexton for many years until his death in 1884, walked with two sticks, which he used to hit the heads of boys misbehaving in the church gallery.

The churchwardens' list includes the names Dagworthy and Wilson, families which have farmed locally for several centuries.

Church and school have defied threats of closure and are now thriving, thanks partly to a growth in population.

A substantial legacy of BTR shares from an "anonymous" maiden lady in 1979 means that the church floor and gallery have been repaired and modern amenities added.

A fascinating history (price £1.50) was compiled by Mr Cedric Iliffe, churchwarden from 1978 to 1990, who in retirement from a career in nuclear engineering has given much to village life. His only other publication, a *History of Atomic Science,* sells at £30!

ST SWITHUN'S, WOODBURY

LOCAL forecasters have a weather eye on Woodbury Church on July 15, for if it rains on St Swithun's Day, tradition claims, it will rain every day for the next 40 days.

The story came about because Swithun, Bishop of Winchester, asked to be buried outside his cathedral "so that the sweet rain from heaven might fall on his grave." When he was made a saint in 971, it was decided to transfer his body into the Cathedral, but the heavens opened in protest and delayed the operation 40 days.

Whatever the weather, parishioners of St Swithun's, Woodbury, proud of their patron saint, celebrate in style on 15 July.

There was evidence of a Saxon church at Woodbury long before St Swithun's time. In his historical notes, a recent Vicar, the Rev David Share, records from an old Anglo-Saxon document: "In Woodbury land, there is another guildship gathered to Christ and St Peter."

The Domesday Book (1086) recorded later: "The King has a Manor called Wodeberie ... of it the Abbot of St Michael's (Normandy) has the Church."

The present building dates from the 13th century, and the 84ft tower, seeming taller on the hilltop, was consecrated in 1409. Fully repaired after a £100,000 appeal in 1994, it houses a ring of eight bells.

Among numerous ancient monuments is a famous epitaph on the north wall: "He first decesed, She for a little tryed to live without him, liked it not and dyed."

A floor tablet records the burial of Henry Pollexfen, MP for Exeter 1688, and Lord Chief Justice of Common Pleas. Although he helped Judge Jeffreys in the notorious assizes after the Monmouth Rebellion (1685), he later proved more merciful in his judgments. He died in 1691.

A little trumpet angel dating from 1777, which stands on top of the organ case, is a favourite with local children, and Woodbury Church School has adopted him for a T-shirt emblem.

Lovely stained glass in the Chantry Chapel on the south side of the nave is 400 years old and thought once to have been in York Minster. This is also called the Drake Chapel, because it contained pews of descendants of Sir Francis Drake, who occupied the parish's Nutwell Court from the 17th century until 1938.

Devon philanthropist Mr G. V. Northcott, of Nutwell Court, completely restored the chapel in 1951. A fine old sea chest is kept in the vestry.

The Churchwarden's Accounts, dating from 1537, record changing fashions, as two items show: 1556 (Queen Mary on throne) For Making image of St Swithun – 14s ...1558 (Queen Elizabeth): For taking down of images and burying them – 14d.

Woodbury's charm is reflected in the long stay of its vicars – at one stage there were only five incumbents covering 200 years.

Vicar for 52 years last century, the Rev John Fulford was responsible for the extensive restoration of the interior and himself repainted the screen in 1863. It has since been regilded and enhanced by Herbert Read Ltd.

Mr Fulford's "high church" style did not please everybody, and a group of parishioners led by Dr Robert Brent built Christ Church, Woodbury's lively Free Church, which has recently been Devon's centre for relief to Romania.

Nowadays the two churches come together regularly for combined worship, including harvest and carols on the Green with Lympstone Marine Band.

People come from far to see the church hassocks faithfully worked from the wildflower drawings of the Rev Dr Keble Martin, who published his famous *Concise British Flora* in retirement at Woodbury. One of two specially bound copies of the book (the other was accepted by the Duke of Edinburgh) was presented to the church by Mrs Martin and is kept in a special oak case in the nave.

CHURCH OF THE NATIVITY OF THE BLESSED VIRGIN, LYMPSTONE

VISITORS are lyrical in their praise of the view across the Exe estuary from Lympstone towards Powderham Castle and Church, and the heights of Haldon.

But Lympstone's ancient church tower, built of local red sandstone, provided more than a fine view during the Civil War, when it was used successively by Cavaliers and Roundheads to fire their cannons at enemy ships sailing upriver to take part in the siege of Exeter.

A link with worship on this site from the distant past is the old font which now rests in dignified retirement at the west end of the north aisle, with this inscription: "This damaged font bowl comes from Saxon times and was used in successive churches until 1864, when it was replaced by the present font. The cable moulding with which it was decorated was cut with an axe, not a chisel."

Norman patrons were the Albemarles. Documents of 1244 and 1274 recorded that Reginald Albemarle was expected to provide horses and bows and arrows for the King "whenever he hunted in the forests of Dartmoor."

The Albemarles and their successors, the Bonvilles, were responsible for the rebuilding of the church in the 14th century. It was finally re-consecrated by Bishop Stafford in 1409 and given the dedication (thought to be unique in England) – The Church of the Nativity of the Blessed Virgin Mary.

A tombstone in memory of Henry Drake in the main aisle is a reminder that the great seafaring family occupied Nutwell Court, where in 1938 after a fire at Buckland Abbey, relics of Sir Francis were housed, including Drake's Drum. Sir Henry Newbolt's rhyme is familiar: "Take my drum to England, hang it by the shore; strike it when your powder's running low..."

Members of the family were buried in the north aisle.

There is a bust in the belfry of grocer Nicholas Lee, three times Mayor of Exeter and "guardian of the poor." He bought the patronage and appointed his son, John Lee, as rector in 1733.

Raising funds is always on the church's agenda. In 1796 Mary Bass (among others) paid two guineas so that she and her descendants "could hold and enjoy a pew for 99 years."

The church was restored and extended in 1833 at the expense of John Bartholomew, who was both rector 1820–40 and Archdeacon of Barnstaple. After more repairs the church was reconsecrated in 1864 by the Bishop of Jamaica, the Rt Rev George Tozer, then acting as assistant to Bishop Phillpotts.

Dedicated in 1938, the east window was given by Admiral Arthur Peters, whose family lived at Harefield, now St Peter's School. Five other stained-glass windows in the church had previously been given by the family.

In 1902, the bells cast in 1746 were rehung and a treble added, making a peal of six to mark Edward VII's Coronation.

Recently Lympstone parishioners have established links to help two villages and their churches in Romania.

POINT-IN-VIEW CHURCH, EXMOUTH

FROM a quiet green field, the church aptly named Point-in-View looks out over Exmouth and the Exe Estuary towards the sea.

With a history as picturesque as its situation, the little building is filled with worshippers on Sundays and attracts visitors from all over the world.

Misses Jane and Mary Parminter, the wealthy cousins who in 1798 built their curious A La Ronde home, now a National Trust property, were members of a gifted North Devon Huguenot family.

As they began to find difficult the journey to Exmouth Congregational Church, they decided to build a chapel on their own 15 acres, within strolling distance of A La Ronde.

It was completed in 1811, only just in time for the elder lady to be buried there, with the inscription: "Here sleeps in Jesus, Miss Jane Parminter. She committed her spirit into the hands of God the Redeemer 6th Nov 1811."

A trust deed then drawn up by her cousin, as executrix, entitled the Mary Parminter Trust, provided for a resident minister, and accommodation for four single women "of approved character and over 50 years of age," one to act as schoolmistress for six poor female children – "the children of Jewish parents in all cases to be preferred." That was the clue to the double meaning of the title "Point-in-View."

The Parminters were caught up in a latterday crusade, which found its expression with the formation in 1809 of the London Society for Promoting Christianity Among the Jews. Later known as the London Jews Society, it greatly influenced Victorian statesmen to promote the eventual foundation of the present State of Israel.

The Parminters planted trees, still growing by their home and chapel, with the written proviso: "These oaks shall remain standing and the hand of man shall not be raised against them till Israel returns and is restored to the Land of Promise." It seems the trees themselves, in those days before iron hulls, were destined to provide timber for ships to transport Jewish settlers to Israel.

There have been necessary changes over the years, but eight trustees continue to administer the trust, which has been augmented by other gifts and today still provides the manse for a retired minister and homes for elderly people. The school closed early this century. The trust status gives Point-in-View an independence, and the thriving congregation is composed of people of all ages and denominations, including two retired ministers of Baptist and Methodist churches.

Many of the numerous couples married at this lovely and unique church keep their allegiance over the years.

HOLY TRINITY CHURCH, EXMOUTH

PINNACLES on the tall tower of Holy Trinity, Exmouth, have made a spectacular landmark from land and sea for almost a century. In early days there was only a chapel of ease here, under the care of Littleham parish church, to serve a small village of fishing folk and those who manned the Exe ferry.

By a document of 1265, the Abbot of Sherborne, Lord of the Manor in medieval times, made agreement with Exeter City that he and his servants or baggage should have free passage on the ferry between Exmouth, or "Checkstones", and Starcross, Checkstones being two rocks at the entrance to the harbour.

Although there were earlier references to chapels in the area, Holy Trinity was first mentioned by name when it was licensed by Bishop Stafford in 1412.

Historian Beatrix Cresswell believes that the chapel was built at the request of the Exmouth villagers, rather than the Vicar of Littleham, who insisted the mother church was attended on festival days and Sundays.

As well as weekday services, in 1648 there were regular lectures – popular entertainment in those days.

But in 1656 the Devon Session Rolls Court heard that the chapel was in a sad state of ruin and decay, "the lead which covered the same being cut off and the timber work destroyed; but because of the decay in fishing and other misfortunes, they were much impoverished and unable to undergo the great costs."

The remedy was to impose a church rate for the repairs.

With a non-resident priest, the chapel's fortunes continued at a low ebb until 1777, when the first Free Church was established at Exmouth by Viscountess Wilhelmina Glenorchy.

Although the little town was described as "too wicked for evangelism," the Glenorchy Church flourished, so that supporters of Holy Trinity Chapel were spurred into action.

In 1799 the old building was replaced by a new one consecrated by Bishop John Ross. As the population grew, in 1824, Lord Rolle, of Littleham Manor, built another church on a site given by him nearby, on the understanding that those who had attended the old chapel were allotted appropriate seats in the new.

Devon's famous composer, Samuel Sebastian Wesley, organist of Exeter Cathedral 1835–41, combined that post with organist of Holy Trinity, Exmouth, in 1837. For £10 a year he was to play for Sunday Evensong and hold a weekly choir practice. The temperamental musician held the post for only one year.

The generosity of the Hon Mark Rolle enabled the extension of the building to create " a stately and effective church" in 1907, when the tower was adorned with a parapet table and 12 crocketed pinnacles.

The destruction of stained-glass windows in the Second World War led to the dedication in 1957 of the first known portrait in stained glass of Winston Churchill. The church furnishings had earlier been enriched by the work of Herbert Read and Harry Hems.

A revised history of the church described the 'recent' interior alterations as "bringing under one roof a multi-functional building in keeping with existing architecture and in line with modern day needs."

ST JOHN-IN-THE-WILDERNESS CHURCH, WITHYCOMBE RALEIGH

THREATENED for centuries with redundancy, like many of today's churches, St John-in-the-Wilderness, Withycombe Raleigh, is defying the past with a renewed spiritual life and an appeal for £250,000.

Taking its "wilderness" title from nearby Woodbury Common, the church dedicated to St John the Baptist, who ministered in desert places, was until 1852 part of East Budleigh parish, and from Norman times served a rural community.

W. G. Hoskins observed memorials to the Raleighs and Drakes "who formerly lived here" – not surprising with the sea so close. Sir Walter's father once owned Withycombe Manor, but the great Raleigh was born at Hayes Barton, three miles away.

The building's early foundation was confirmed with the discovery of Norman works when the church was repaired this century, and there is a 15th-century font, marking the date of the origins of the present structure.

First record of a "chapel in Wydcomb" is in the 13th century, when it was connected by Church Lane to the manor, now known as Withycombe Barton.

But while the population in Withycombe village grew, people found St John-in-the-Wilderness too remote, and St Michael's chapel, now the site of the school, was built; so for 300 years St John's was regarded as very much "in the wilds", used mainly for burials and other occasional services. The neglected building fell into disrepair.

In 1688 the churchwardens reported that the church was "much dilapidated", and in 1788 the Vicar of East Budleigh wanted it demolished, but the tower and north aisle were saved.

Exmouth grew in the 19th century in two sections, Littleham parish and Withycombe village. In 1852 Bishop Phillpotts granted Withycombe parish status, separating it from East Budleigh.

For 12 years St John-in-the-Wilderness was the parish church until the opening in 1864 in the village centre of the big new church of St John the Evangelist.

Still on the outskirts of Exmouth, the Wilderness church survived, was renovated between 1926 and 1936, and now finds itself in the centre of a sea of houses. People returned to St John in his wilderness, and the threat of redundancy is gone.

Bosses in the renewed chancel have the rare image of uncrowned Edward VIII, who abdicated just after the church's re-dedication in 1936.

Two well-known Victorian artists are buried here. They were Irish-born landscape painter, Francis Danby, who spent the last 20 years of his eventful life in Exmouth, and William Holwell Carr, artist Vicar of Menheniot in Cornwall, whose parents lived in the parish.

Visiting the church in 1939, Arthur Mee met Arthur Wilmot, aged 90, who had been 80 years in the choir, and his son, Raymond, 40 years an organist.

LITTLEHAM

SEA AIR pervades the Church of St Margaret and St Andrew, Littleham. The ceiling plaster was removed about 100 years ago to reveal a spectacular roof which brings to mind the interior of a timber-built boat.

In the area rightly called "the nave" which the now restored roof covers, an elegant memorial reads: "Viscountess Nelson, Duchess of Bronti, widow of the late Viscount Nelson, and her son, Josiah Nisbet Esq. Captain RN."

Lady Nelson's tomb in the churchyard attracts so many visitors that special stepping stones have been placed to it from the main path.

Captain Nesbit, son of Lady Nelson's first husband – a doctor in the West Indies – served in his stepfather's fleet. Lady Nelson, widowed a second time at Trafalgar, moved from Bath to The Beacon, Exmouth. It seems she spent her last years in comfort, while Lady Hamilton died in poverty in Calais.

Another grave nearby surrounded by anchors is a sign that seafarers of all kinds, including admirals, are buried in the vast 12-acre churchyard.

One such was Christopher Nesham, a native of Exmouth, who became Admiral in 1852 after 70 years in the Royal Navy.

Following the sea theme, the name "Drake aisle" given to the north side of the church falls neatly into the pattern. It was added to the main aisle by the family in 1528.

Joan, sister of Gilbert Drake, churchwarden for many years, married Walter Raleigh, of East Budleigh, who was father of the famous Sir Walter by a later marriage.

The church, which celebrated its 750th anniversary in style a few years ago, was built on the site of earlier churches.

Churchwarden Mrs Yvonne Wardrop pointed with pride to the Saxon scratch dial, or Mass clock, now discreetly incorporated into the outer wall of the present building. It used to indicate the times of service to the parishioners.

It was the first recorded Vicar, Roger de Littleham, who started building the present church in 1231 on the site of an earlier structure.

The lectern deserves a second glance. It was carved in 1884 from a beam which for some reason had been rejected from Salisbury Cathedral in 1250.

How many angels can be found in the building? It is a question asked of generations of Sunday School pupils by Miss Geraldine Sharp.

Carved, painted, or in stained-glass windows, angels are indeed to be observed on all sides. There are said to be at least 100 of them.

The parish of Littleham-cum-Exmouth is linked with Trinity Church in the town centre.

ST PETER'S, BUDLEIGH SALTERTON

THE SPACIOUS interior of St Peter's, Budleigh Salterton, makes it an ideal venue for special occasions, of which many were planned in 1993 to mark the church's centennial.

The town itself grew from an early settlement of a few salt workers' and fishermen's huts on the sea front. Because of the salt pans at the river estuary, it was called "Salterton", a name still used by local people to distinguish it from "Budleigh", which is now usually known as East Budleigh.

It was when the beauty spot was "discovered" by a number of wealthy families, who built large seaside homes in the mid-18th century, that it took a new identity, losing its reputation as a smugglers' paradise.

The first church, Holy Trinity, a chapel of ease to the East Budleigh parish church, was built in 1813.

Early residents who supported church life included the romantic Torriano family, descendants of a Protestant Italian count and Christian minister, who fled from religious persecution by the Austrian Emperor.

Another resident, Sir John Millais, used the shore as a setting for the famous picture, Boyhood of Raleigh, portraying the young Sir Walter with his half-brother, Humphrey Gilbert.

As the population grew, the Hon Mark Rolle, owner of Bicton Manor and younger brother of the 20th Lord Clinton, decided that provision of a larger church was overdue.

It was mainly through his generosity that St Peter's arose. It would have been even more majestic had the original plan for a tower with a 140ft spire been completed.

Alarmed at the estimated costs when the plans first appeared, the Rev Rees Price, curate, warned Mark Rolle that "there is not much wealth in the parish except for two or three families"; but the work went ahead, the main contributors besides the Hon Mark being his sister-in-law, Lady Alice Ewing, and a retired clergyman, the Rev James Boucher, who was also the principal founder of the town hospital.

Known for his generosity, Mr Boucher always responded when approached by poor people by giving them food vouchers to be used at the town coffee house.

The new church was consecrated by Bishop Bickersteth of Exeter on April 25, 1893, and Budleigh Salterton became a separate parish in 1900, with Mark Rolle as patron and Rees Price as the first vicar.

St Peter's was badly damaged by a German bomb in 1942. While temporary repairs were effected, the congregation was made welcome at the Methodist Church. Although nobody was killed in that raid, the church war memorial records the names of 10 civilians who lost their lives between 1939 and 1945.

During Canon Kenneth Parry's time, a nave organ from Worcester Cathedral was installed to supplement the church's own instrument.

ALL SAINTS, EAST BUDLEIGH

TRICK or treat visits are hardly warranted in East Budleigh, for on each November 1, by tradition, children stand under the tower of All Saints Church to catch buns thrown by the Vicar.

The custom began more than 300 years ago when a local woman was so overjoyed by the arrival

of William of Orange at Brixham that she gave buns each year to the parish children.

Walter Raleigh, a churchwarden's son born at Hayes Barton Farm in 1552, regularly attended the church and received his first schooling from Vicar John Ford.

In 1984, to celebrate the 400th anniversary of Sir Walter's founding of North Carolina (with its capital city Raleigh), a large contingent of Americans attended special services at East Budleigh Church and Exeter Cathedral.

The memorial to Joan Raleigh, herself a member of the seafaring Drake family, is in the nave near the Raleigh pew. She was the first of the three wives of Sir Walter Raleigh's father.

Sir Walter's portrait, painted anonymously by a well-known artist who retired to Devon, is on the north wall, with a shield of HMS *Raleigh*, which keeps close links with the church.

In King Alfred's time, East Budleigh, or Bodelia as it was then named, was the Royal centre of the "hundred", or ancient district, of what is now known as East Devon.

It remained a thriving port until the Otter Estuary filled with river silt in medieval times.

Repairs to the church in the last century revealed Saxon stonework, indicating that the fine hill site has been a centre of worship from early times.

The nave is noted for a unique set of carved pew-ends, mostly 400 years old. Two of these reveal further New World links. A Red Indian head was probably carved by a sailor on his return from America.

The coat of arms on another bench is of the local Conant family. In 1623 Roger Conant became a founder citizen of Massachusetts and Salem City, famed for the witches' trials of 1692. A wheel from a mill on the Conants' farm is mounted in concrete outside the church hall. Residents have resisted pleas to sell it to their American "cousins".

A much-loved Vicar of 58 years (1794–1852), Ambrose Stapleton, besides being a brilliant preacher, organised the smuggling activities which were common practice in those times. No less than five memorials on the south wall record the names of 10 members of the Stapleton family.

A current church history records that galleries erected in the last century to include worshippers from the growing population at Budleigh Salterton were later taken down when the town became a separate parish and built its own church.

A window showing Christ calming the waters is in memory of Admiral Preedy, Captain of the *Agamemnon*, which laid the first cable linking America and Britain.

Medieval bosses in the 15th-century wagon roof, two early glass coats of arms, and 250 modern hand-worked kneelers help to make All Saints one of Devon's loveliest churches.

ST MARY'S, BICTON

PERHAPS it was typical of Victorian values that Devon's richest woman in the 19th century should devote much of her great wealth to support local church life.

Young Louisa Trefusis, daughter of the 19th Baron Clinton, married in 1920 Lord John Rolle, then 64, and they lived in Bicton Manor, which had been splendidly rebuilt in 1730. André Le Nôtre, of Versailles fame, was commissioned to lay out the Bicton Gardens.

Widowed in 1842, Lady Rolle decided to build a new church in her husband's memory. As a lavish contemporary book explained: "Desirous of erecting a lasting memorial of her deceased husband, as well as devoting part of her wealth to the glory of God, Lady Rolle, entirely at her own cost has brought to completion the building of a new church in the parish of Bicton to take the place of the old church, which from age had greatly dilapidated."

In fact it is open to question whether the old church, its ruins still standing next to the Victorian building, was really beyond repair.

The Domesday Book tells of a Saxon church on the site, with Godo as priest, just before the Norman Conquest.

A well-preserved family tomb among the ruins includes marble likenesses of Denys Rolle, who died at 24 in 1638, his finely dressed wife, and their son, aged five.

Lady Rolle's church, designed by the famous Exonian, Haywood, has a unique feature on the outside walls. On the window dripstones are carved all the Kings and Queens of England, starting from Edward I and his Queen Eleanor and ending with Queen Victoria and Prince Albert. Henry VIII is paired with Katherine of Aragon, and Edward VI with his mother Jane Seymour; Henry's other four wives are not recorded.

One authority says that the heads, 52 in all, are good likenesses. Lord and Lady Rolle were included among the Royals in the north side, overlooking their lovely gardens.

In fact, all reigning monarchs from Queen Victoria to George VI have worshipped here, and hopes are high that the present Queen will attend the 150th anniversary in AD 2000.

On the south side of the impressive interior is a modern stained-glass window given by Mr Noel James, MC OBE, in memory of his wife and six-year-old son. Churchwarden until his death in 1994, Mr James was land agent for the Clinton estates (formerly Rolle) and a world expert on trees. His books include *A History of English Forestry*.

It may be said of him and the Rolles "if you seek their memorial look around you", for the church, secluded from the gardens and accessible only by an inconspicuous road, is surrounded by many beautiful and exotic trees.

A gem set in this secluded leafy island, the church has sometimes been threatened with redundancy, but Churchwarden Mike George and his wife Sandra head a dedicated congregation determined to keep it open.

Lady Rolle, still remembered in vivid local verbal tradition as being driven by liveried postillions in a coach and four to Sunday worship, says "Amen" to that.

ST MICHAEL, OTTERTON

A PERFECT site to settle: that must have been the thought of those who first made Otterton their home; and it was a long time ago, because the word "otter" meaning "water" is Celtic.

When the Saxons took over, they saw no reason to move the village, situated a mile inland from the river estuary and out of harm's way from marauding Danish seafarers.

Saxons probably built the first church on the hill, but their peace was shattered when King Harold, son of Countess Gytha, who owned Otterton Manor, was killed at Hastings.

The extensive Otterton Manor lands, which then included Sidmouth, Venn Ottery, and Harpford, were made as a rich gift by William the Conqueror to his friends, the monks of St Michel Monastery, Normandy, who had helped his invasion, not just with prayers but also with ships.

An abbot and about four monks came and built a daughter abbey at Otterton, and their sturdy tower, recently renovated, forms part of the present church building.

The monks had an active and happy life. They fished in the Otter estuary, which then covered a much wider area than now, and shipped the manor's wool to the Continent from Bankly Wharf. The prior employed 33 salt workers at "Salterton" (now Budleigh Salterton). Part of their building still exists, reshaped, in four houses.

A record book of the priory made in 1259 is now in the possession of Lord Coleridge, of Ottery St Mary.

The manor was bought from the Church in Henry VIII's time by the Dukes, a local family. When in 1553 the Estuary began to silt up, Richard Duke tried to clear a way for shipping.

The churches of Otterton, East Budleigh, and Sidmouth each sold a bell from their towers to help pay for the work, the Otterton bell being bought for £10 by Walter Raleigh (father of Sir Walter), of Hayes Barton.

The estuary finally became unusable from 1778, when a last load of stone was unshipped at Bankly Wharf.

Disaster struck the Rev Richard Venn, a local lad who had succeeded his father as Vicar of Otterton in 1625, when at the age of 44 he was imprisoned by Roundhead troops on 23 December 1645. He and his wife and their 11 children were evicted from their home and lived in dire poverty, often separated, for the next 15 years.

Meanwhile an East Budleigh Presbyterian minister, Richard Conant, was installed at the Otterton Church, and remained there until Mr Venn was reinstated in 1660. Venn lived just another two years, but Conant turned Anglican and became Vicar of East Budleigh in 1672.

Centuries later, descendants of Mr Venn arranged for a marble tablet in his memory to be placed on the north wall above the choirstalls.

The Rolle family, of Bicton and Stevenstone, bought Otterton manor in 1785. When Lord John Rolle died in 1842 he left his widow, Lady Louisa Rolle (daughter of Lord Clinton) a large fortune. In 1871 she replaced the derelict main body of the church with the present building, all at her own expense.

Why is it so big? Lady Rolle expected everyone in the parish church on Sunday and put as much pressure as she could on local people, irrespective of denomination, to attend services.

Pupils from far and wide were given incentives to attend Sunday School, which she herself ran. Each child who during the week learned by heart a selected passage of Scripture was awarded a threepenny bit (3d); as a consequence generations of pupils who attended Lady Rolle's classes were noted as having the best knowledge of the Bible in all East Devon.

Around the Churches of East Devon

Otterton's church history has been well recorded in recent years by Mr Michael Harrison and by Miss Mary Brimblecombe. A direct link with the rebuilding of the church was provided by Miss Ethel Smith, of 20 Fore Street, who related how her grandfather supplied horses and wagons free to haul the stone onto the site.

The Norman connection was renewed when Otterton twinned with the French town of Vieux.

ST JOHN THE BAPTIST CHURCH, COLATON RALEIGH

THE FAMOUS Raleigh family left a permanent mark in East Devon in the names of two parishes where they owned manors – Colaton Raleigh and Withycombe Raleigh.

As the original name "Cola's ton" implies, there was a large enclosed settlement in Saxon times, and in the Domesday survey "Coletona" was Royal property.

When later Henry I exchanged the manor for Topsham, part of the land was acquired by the immensely wealthy William Brewer, a signatory of Magna Carta, founder in 1196 of the Torre (Torquay) Abbey and also Dunkeswell Abbey, and generally noted for his generosity to the Church. His widow described herself as Domina Coletona.

Later a "Raleghe" of Somerset gained a share of this property by marriage. In 1346 Peter de Raleghe and the Abbot of Dunkeswell shared manor rights, and the family name was affixed forever to the parish.

The church, however, was provided for by another property which appears to have been left by Brewer to his nephew, also William Brewer, Bishop of Exeter 1224 to 1244. When he went to the Crusades, Bishop Brewer appointed a dean and gave him the property and the church as an endowment. It is thought that this dean or a successor built a new church of local sandstone.

The deans also built for themselves a substantial home nearby, now known as Place Court, with its own chapel.

In this St Michael's chapel Sir Walter Raleigh, born at Hayes Barton, East Budleigh, is thought to have been baptised.

The deans' interest continued. A register records: "The Rev Dr Charles Lyttleton, Dean of Exon, sent a silver paten which formerly belonged to St Michael's chapel within the Deanery House to the Church of Colaton 'Rawleigh' for use in the Lord's Supper. Given May 27, 1749."

Earlier Dean Gregory Dobbs (1560–70) gave the church a fine Elizabethan silver tazza (shallow cup) with the familiar deanery crest of a stag's head engraved upon it.

A "tithe sheaf" of a nearby property, Bystock, was given as part of the vicar's income from as early as 1269. One tradition says that this sheaf was formerly paid to the Vicar of East Budleigh, but he failed to visit the manor during a plague, so the sheaf was thereafter given to the vicar of Colaton Raleigh, who had stepped in to care for the people.

Another faithful pastor was Vicar James Hobbs, who "resided among his parishioners" 50 years at a time when so many incumbents were "absentee landlords". He died in 1809.

Although the church retains a Norman font and the tower is 15th century, it was extensively rebuilt last century.

A feature of great interest to artists is the series of murals made in the style of "sgraffito" – a medieval Italian method using coloured plaster.

Evidence of the church's role in promoting education is inscribed on the old school building, now the village hall: "Erected by subscription under Anthony Greenwood Vicar 1840.

"Train a child in the way he should go, and when he is old he will not depart from it." A message that maybe needs re-learning today.

Colaton Raleigh is now attached to Newton Poppleford.

ST GREGORY'S CHURCH, HARPFORD

THATCHED homes and woodlands providing a concert hall for the melody of a thousand birds make an ideal setting for St Gregory's Church, Harpford.

Nobody who had descended straight from the sky into the churchyard, and looked over the peaceful section of the River Otter below, would imagine that the busy Exeter–Sidmouth road runs through Newton Poppleford less than a mile away.

The inscription on a memorial in the church rings as true today as it did a century ago. "Sir James Walker died 1885 aged 76. Governor of Barbados, 50 years of service at home and abroad ... came down here to find rest and retirement, and found it."

Meaning perhaps "ford of the musical stream", Harpford may have been a settlement in Roman times. Villagers certainly lived and worshipped here before the Conquest, and Saxon and Norman kings had the gift of the manor.

A deed of 31 August 1206, confirmed the gift a year earlier by Bishop Marshall of Exeter of the parish of Harpford and the chapel of Venn Ottery to the Abbey of St Michel, Normandy, which had already established a cell at Otterton, two miles down river.

First named vicar appointed from Otterton under this contract was Gilbert de Endwreth.

He was installed by Henry de Molensis, Archdeacon of Exeter, in 1208, in the absence of a bishop; during the turbulent years of King John, no Bishop of Exeter was appointed between the death of Bishop John Marshall in 1206 and the installation of Simon of Apulia in 1214.

The next named vicar in 1272 was local – Adam of "Clist St Mary".

Patron saint of both Harpford and Venn Ottery churches is St Gregory the Great. Only two other Devon parish churches are dedicated to him.

As festivals of patron saints were of great importance in medieval times, the vicar of the two churches in 1419 was given permission by Bishop Stafford to avoid a clash by changing the Venn Ottery festival from 12 March to 10 December.

George Arthur, appointed vicar in 1551, was deprived when Queen Mary came to the throne in 1553, but after two intervening vicars, was restored in 1560. Until his death in 1583, he took no less than 236 weddings at Harpford – many of them couples from other parishes. The splendid local guide rightly asks: "Was Harpford a local Gretna Green?"

The celebrated young hymnwriter of "Rock of Ages", Augustus Toplady, vicar 1766–68, was given the "country cure for the good of his health" before transferring to Broadhembury.

His memory was perpetuated in 1913 by the restoration of the ancient churchyard cross by craftsman Harry Hems, with words from the famous hymn inscribed: "Nothing in my hand I bring, simply to Thy cross I cling."

OTTERY ST MARY CHURCH

OFTEN described as the finest parish church in Devon, Ottery St Mary has two clocks, both of them working. One has its obvious place in the tower. The other, inside the building, is of great historic interest, being built in 1340 at the order of Bishop Grandisson, a native of Switzerland, a sign that the Swiss love of clocks goes back a long time.

Similar clocks, whose design is based on the belief that the Earth was the centre of the Solar System, were also built in Exeter Cathedral 1318, Wimborne Minster 1320, and Wells Cathedral 1326.

John de Grandisson, Bishop of Exeter 1327–69, also rebuilt Ottery Church in a similar pattern to Exeter Cathedral and in 1338 founded the school, which in Henry VIII's time was renamed the "Kynges Newe Grammar Scole of Seynt Marie Oterey," according to Mr John Whitham's church history.

Grandisson also established a college of secular canons, so that it was known as the Collegiate Church of Ottery St Mary.

This was changed by Henry VIII to a College of Governors, known as the Church Corporation, who were to "have succession forever." So far the king's decree holds good.

Around the Churches of East Devon

Among recent chairman of the governors is Mr Oliver William-Powlett, whose family home at Cadhay two miles away is one of Devon's finest historic country houses.

Besides being a remarkable medieval building, the church attracts visitors from all over the world because of its association with the poet Samuel Taylor Coleridge.

The poet's image on an outside church wall-plaque is accompanied by words from *The Ancient Mariner*: "He prayeth best who loveth best all things both great and small." He was the 13th child of the Vicar, who from 1760 to 1781 bemused his parishioners with long Bible quotations in Hebrew and Greek from the pulpit.

As a small boy, Samuel caused an all-night search by the townsfolk when he wandered off on his own. Eventually he was found on the banks of the Otter.

Inside, memorials record the leading legal role of the Coleridge family in Victorian England. The present Lord Coleridge occupies the family home, Chanter's House, next to the church.

The great Anglican martyr of last century, Bishop John Coleridge Patteson, was son of Frances Duke Coleridge, another member of the Ottery family. After being curate at Alfington in the parish of Ottery he served courageously in the South Seas until at Nukapu Island on 20 September 1871, "his life was taken by men for whom he would gladly have given it."

The parish register of June 1750 records the baptism of Joanna Southcott. Daughter of a Gittisham farmer, her prophecies about the end of the world are still sought in occult circles.

Thinking herself to be the woman of Revelations 12, at 64 she announced she was to give birth to the Prince of Peace.

Her death soon afterwards has not silenced rumours about boxes of prophecies she left, but one of them opened in 1927 revealed nothing significant.

Church music – ancient and modern – has been a central feature of parish life. Michael Farley has earned a reputation for excellence in the West Country and beyond both as organist and as an organ builder. The church's splendid instrument has been in good hands.

OTTERY ST MARY UNITED REFORMED CHURCH
DESCRIBED in 1897 by the Lord Chief Justice, Lord Coleridge, of Ottery St Mary, as one of the oldest Nonconformist places of worship in Britain, the first Ottery St Mary Congregational (now United Reformed) Church was built in 1688.

His assessment of the building still in Jesu Street is appropriate to this day: "This old world house of prayer is both historically and artistically a charming feature of the town."

There is a link between the church and Chanter's House. For some centuries now the home of the Coleridge family, in the turbulent days of Oliver Cromwell and Charles II the estate belonged to the Rev Robert Collins, the church's first minister, who inherited it from his father.

Cromwell himself once stayed there, and in the "Great Parlour" Sir John Fairfax received "a fair jewel set with diamonds of great value" for his victory at Naseby.

When Charles II came to the throne in 1660, and Nonconformist worshippers were compelled to go underground, Robert Collins, ousted from his post as Rector of Talaton, resumed residence at Chanter's House and held secret services there, within a stone's throw of Ottery parish church.

The authorities made many attempts to prevent this, and in 1670 churchwardens, constables, and a "great mob" raided the house during a service.

Robert Collins was arrested and later fined £40 by Sir Peter Prideaux, of Netherton Hall, Farway.

Collins persisted with the "illegal" worship, but after further destructive raids led by Squire Nicholas Haydon, of nearby Cadhay, and a prison sentence in Exeter, he sold Chanter's House and went with his family to Holland, where he was free to worship as he pleased.

Returning to Ottery in 1690, he preached there unharmed until his death in 1697.

Local historian Mrs Gladys Tucker recorded that the Rev John Walrond, who succeeded him as minister in 1698, was engaged in a theological battle with an Exeter Unitarian movement, which denied that Jesus was the Son of God. Eventually two Exeter ministers were expelled, and the campaign "to diminish Jesus Christ into a legend" faded.

There is a tradition that, in common with other Nonconformist churches of early times, the first Ottery meeting house once had a trapdoor near the pulpit, so that the minister could escape if a constable appeared.

The original pulpit and box pews were removed last century. The clock, made by John Pepys, of London, between 1680 and 1708, is still there. It is wound each week, but the hourly chime was stopped long ago, because it irritated the preachers when in full flow.

Added in 1878, at the turn of the century the school room accommodated two Sunday School sessions, with 200 children and 22 teachers.

ST ANDREW'S, FENITON

FENITON'S place in Devon's history is firmly established as the boyhood home of John Patteson (1827–1871), pioneer missionary, martyr, and first Bishop of Melanesia in the Pacific.

His memorial is a familiar landmark on the A30 at a crossroad linking Feniton and Ottery St Mary, and there is a Patteson Chapel in St Andrew's Church, Feniton, with a wooden cross, the gift of what is now the Archdiocese of Melanesia.

The bishop's father, Judge Sir John Patteson, and his mother, Frances, a member of the Coleridge family of Ottery St Mary, lived at the ancient manor, Feniton Court.

Set snugly in a sheltered site beside the great house, St Andrew's was built in the 15th century by the Norman Malherbe family, who were lords of the manor for 300 years.

The Rev Henry Watson, rector between the two world wars, in his carefully researched history of the village, believed that there was an earlier building "on a curious bit of rising ground between the present church and the road."

In the time of John Pring, rector 1525–1558, the field near Fenny Bridges known as "Bloody Meadow" was the scene of the first battle in 1549 between Lord Russell's Royal Army and the South-West forces of the Prayer Book Rebellion. Up to 1,000 rebels lost their lives that day.

Russell's chaplain, Miles Coverdale, was already famous as translator of one of the first Bibles in English.

Around the Churches of East Devon

He was made Bishop of Exeter two years later, only to be forced into exile on Queen Mary's accession in 1553. Living through such troubled times, it was natural for John Pring to choose the inscription on his church tomb: "Prepare for Death."

A century later, Charles Churchill, a man with a florid complexion and hearty laugh, also found life far from dull. He survived as rector during Cromwell's rule from 1642 until 1657, when he was expelled with his wife and four children to Somerset on trumped-up charges – of being addicted to "licquor" (florid countenance), allowing his children to play cards for pins, and being a "notorious cavalier".

Restored on Charles II's accession in 1660, he lived on as rector for another 30 years.

Churchwarden's accounts give a background to parish life. In 1693 it is recorded: "Spent upon ringers the 5th of November and at other rejoicing days 12s which ye pishoners (parishioners) looks upon to be too much and very extravigent and hardly allowed it."

An entry of 1695 suggests the wardens had changed: "Spent ye 5th November in commemoration of ye damnable powder plot and hellish conspiracy of ye papists 7s."

At pauper funerals "sider and bread" or "cakes and ale" were provided for the bearers.

The screen may have come from Dunkeswell Abbey, when it was demolished in 1536; and following a hobby of many Victorian women, Mrs Hart, wife of William Hart (rector 1899–1918) carved the lectern.

As the earliest rectors were Norman, it is fitting that the porch proudly displays the parish's twinning charter with Louvigny in Calvados in 1976.

ST MARY'S CHURCH, WHIMPLE

DISCREETLY cushioned by a mile of countryside from the busy A30, the village of Whimple, with St Mary's Church at its heart, gladdens the eye of the refugee from city stress.

The name itself, meaning in Celtic "White Pool", suggests that even after the Saxon invasion 1,300 years ago, the British settlement was left mainly undisturbed. It is also thought that the first church was of timber and Saxon built.

After the Danes were deprived of Exeter partly by the courage of Pinhoe's vicar in 1001, it is likely that they moved east and ravaged Whimple's church and farmsteads.

Permanent change came with the Norman Conquest, and Domesday records show that manor and church advowson were granted to the powerful Sheriff of Devon, Baldwin, whose descendants later bestowed Whimple on the Prior and Convent of Cowick, Exeter, a branch of the great Benedictine Abbey of Bec in Normandy. First recorded Rector in 1258, William Pincerna occupied the original Norman stone church.

One of the most interesting features is the medieval panel portrait of Henry VI, once part of a chancel screen, later used as a pulpit step, and since 1955 placed with seven other unique portraits at the west end. "Saintly" young Henry carried on the war with France of his famous father Henry V.

The incomes of all French-controlled monasteries, like Cowick, were seized to support the war effort.

Beatrix Cresswell noted that Henry VI and the Cowick Prior were in dispute over the rights to Whimple, and a lawsuit was heard in St Mary Major Church, which stood until 1974 in front of Exeter Cathedral.

The decision favoured the prior, because the king was no longer at war with France – where after the uprising of Joan of Arc, eventually only Calais remained in English hands.

But five years later the Crown had its way when Cowick's last prior yielded the parish to the king, who between 1451 and 1464 used Whimple's revenues to help finance his new foundations, Eton College and King's College, Cambridge. It is thought the king's portrait was painted about this time.

After Henry's murder, his successor, Edward IV, gave the parish to Tavistock Abbey.

The Earl of Bedford, who took over that abbey at the Dissolution of the Monasteries, appointed William Cotton, son of the Bishop of Exeter, as rector in 1608. He became Archdeacon of Totnes before being driven out by the Roundheads to exile in the family Castle of Bottreany in Cornwall, leaving his curate, John Phare, to suffer persecution .

In what may well be a Devon record, two successive rectors ran the parish for 113 years. Canon Thos. Heberden, rector 1786–1843 (nearly 57 years) also resided at Exeter Cathedral.

The Rev Lloyd Sanders, rector 1843–1899, rebuilt the church except for the tower in 1846, and was followed by his son, Andrew (rector 1899–1928).

The oldest of the six bells in the tower has the Latin inscription "Holy Mary, tender maiden, protect those I call together." The bells were silent for a time before 1924, when a team of women ringers took over and had the peal repaired, rehung, and re-dedicated by Dean Gamble, of Exeter, in 1929.

ST GILES, SIDBURY

POWDER ROOM had a literal meaning when it was used by villagers 200 years ago referring to a small area above the porch at St Giles Church, Sidbury, because gunpowder was stored there by soldiers who were quartered in the area to guard against any invasion during the Napoleonic Wars.

Historian Baring-Gould last century spoke to people who recalled that during the wars local women were given red coats and marched in rows on Castle Hill, carrying broomsticks, to look like a regiment of soldiers if the French invaded.

The Powder Room is now called the Archive Room and houses documents cared for by the honorary church archivists, Barbara and Alan Softly, who are currently compiling a photo album, *Sidbury Past.*

And Sidbury – parish, village, and church – does indeed have as interesting a past as any place in Devon.

On Sidbury Hill neolithic remains have been found of a camp c. 4,000 BC, and Sidbury Castle is an Iron Age fort built c. 200 BC by Celts fleeing from the Romans in Brittany. This gave the village its name – Sid-burgh – fort on the Sid.

Evidence that Saxons built a stone church some time after their arrival in the 7th century was found in the discovery in 1898 of a Saxon crypt – unique in Devon and one of only six in Britain. On permanent display is the imaginative model of the Saxon church by a recent vicar, John Allen.

W.G. Hoskins wrote: "Not a stone of Saxon building remains in Devon except Sidbury crypt and one or two fragments in Exeter."

Features of the Norman building which replaced the Saxon church are apparent in the lovely well-lit interior.

Unusual is the list of churchwardens since 1613, compiled by the Hon Rev H. H. Courtenay, Rector of Powderham, and given by Sir Charles Cave, Bart, churchwarden in 1924.

Freemasons believe that the memorial to John Stone marks him as an early member of their craft. It reads: "An epitaph upon ye life and death of John Stone, Freemason who departed this life ye first of January, 1617. On our Great Corner Stone, this Stone relied..."

Present Vicar John Lee knows how long he has preached because the pulpit faces the large clock placed on the old gallery, which housed musicians before the organ's advent. Given by an earlier vicar, John Fellowes, in 1817, the clock with a loud tick was made by John Murch, of Honiton. Obviously Mr Fellowes needed a reminder when to stop talking.

The vicar's sermons were subject to scrutiny, too, when the parish was officially visited in 1301. Although he was said to be a good preacher and did his duty well, the vicar was criticised for not preaching about mortal sin.

The Church Friends value their lovely building, and care is devoted to future activities as well as past treasures.

ST GILES AND ST NICHOLAS, SIDMOUTH

MAINLY a Victorian reconstruction, Sidmouth Parish Church was honoured with the gift by Queen Victoria herself of the fine West window in memory of her father, the Duke of Kent, who died in the town in 1820.

The duke and duchess retreated to the town, hounded by creditors, and stayed at the Woolbrook Glen, now the Royal Glen Hotel. Just before he died, the duke often took the infant Victoria in his arms down to the beach and proudly showed her to visitors, inviting them to take a special look, "for she is to be your Queen."

The window has some scenes from the life of St Nicholas (Santa Claus), who, because of a miraculous sea rescue, is the patron saint of sailors as well as children.

The first church on the site in Norman (or maybe Saxon) times was dedicated to the popular Frenchman, St Giles. The name of St Nicholas was added when a second church was built and dedicated in 1259 by Bishop Walter Bronescombe, because Sidmouth was then developing as a naval and fishing port.

The church has since been dedicated to both saints.

It was served by vicars appointed by the Prior of the neighbouring village of Otterton, who in turn was subject to the Abbot of Mont St Michel in Normandy. First recorded Vicar, Gulielmus, was instituted in 1175, an event celebrated with a *son et lumière* 800 years later in 1975.

The town supplied three ships and 62 men as part of the English force which fought at Calais and Crécy in 1346, but its importance as a port had died by 1565, when its harbour, like Otterton's, had filled with silt.

After a long period as a small fishing village, Sidmouth's warm winter climate attracted the wealthy, who were barred from the Continent in the Napoleonic Wars. They stayed, built their "cottages" (many now hotels), and their wealth was used to rebuild the church 1859–60.

One of the biggest contributors, the Earl of Buckinghamshire, a vigorous opponent of the High Church movement, stated his case with posters all over the town. His chief memorial is the East window.

The lovely old east window and some ancient stonework were saved at the time by the historian Peter Orlando Hutchinson, and included in his house nearby, called The Old Chancel, still to be seen overlooking the bowling green.

The church's oldest structure is the 15th-century tower, in which three bells were hung in 1445; one remains as a sanctus bell. The present peal of 10 was made up in stages with bells ranging from 1667 to this century.

"Golden Fish" was the nickname of a rich Victorian with a church window in his memory, whose wealth came from 400 public houses. Living at The Knowle, now East Devon Council offices, Thomas Leversedge Fish filled the 40 rooms with art treasures.

There is also a memorial to Sir Ambrose Fleming, died 1945, inventor of the valve used in radio.

When Roundheads stabled their horses in the church, they also removed the organ, and the people worshipped without one for 200 years.

Recently rebuilt, the present organ is renowned as one of the best instruments in the South-West, and world-famous performer Carlo Curley has played here during the annual concert season.

ST PETER AND ST MARY CHURCH, SALCOMBE REGIS

CLIFFS more than 500ft high rising from the sea at Salcombe Regis, near Sidmouth, have helped the parish and its lovely church maintain an undisturbed charm.

The name is derived from the salt produced in the swampy Sid estuary long ago. The royal "Regis" – retained to distinguish the parish from Salcombe in the South Hams – comes from its connection 1,000 years past with Saxon King Athelstan, who gave the parish to the Church as "pure alms."

The series of wooded valleys which made up the terrain was not thought to be much of a gift in those days, but the first church was built of local timber in a forest clearing.

In the 12th century the Bishop of Exeter bestowed the property on the Cathedral canons, who built a new church, again from local material – greensand stone, which has also been used in the Cathedral over the centuries.

Part of this church, locally believed to have been raised in 1111, is included in the present structure, including the splendid pillar in front of the pulpit.

When Bishop Stapeldon visited c. 1311, he heard a complaint that the image of the patron saint, the Virgin Mary, had torn and scanty clothing. St Peter's name was added to the dedication when the tower was built in the 15th century.

The 14th-century "bird" lectern, carved from solid oak, has a history of its own.

Hidden, like many other objects from Devon churches, in Cromwell's time, it reappeared in the thatch of Sid Abbey in 1849. The vicar of the day was not impressed: "The eagle they have restored is singularly ugly."

A memorial records the 111 years of Miriam Banister, who was baptised in 1817.

A sad tale attends the death at sea of Robert Lee on September 1, 1761. His father, walking along the shore during a storm to see if any ships were in distress, came upon the body of his son, who he had imagined safely in port. It was the subject of a poem by the Rev John Keble.

Vicar at that time was the Rev Joseph Hall, whose 63 years in office ended with his death in 1791.

Sir Norman Lockyer, founder of the famous observatory built in 1911 on the hill above the church, is also buried in the churchyard. In their heyday, his telescopes led research into colliding meteors and sunspots.

Nearby lies another great scientist, Sir Ambrose Fleming, who developed the thermionic valve used in radio technology.

Herbert Read carved the prayer desk given in memory of a member of a local family, the Cornishes, who was the first Bishop of Madagascar from 1874 to 1905.

One old tomb inscription catches the serenity of the surroundings:

"We wait until the morning when the just shall be wakened out of their dust. Our blest Redeemer will then raise us up, His glorious name to praise."

ST WINIFRED'S, BRANSCOMBE

BRANSCOMBE Church has been likened to a fortress standing guard at the entry to one of Devon's most beautiful valleys. Was the valley's name originally Brannoc's Combe? If so, the Welsh saint of that name may have preached here before AD 600.

The church's dedication to another Welsh Christian, Winifred, patron saint of virgins, raises hope that the National Trust, which now owns the Branscombe shoreline, with cliffs 400 and 500ft on either side, will preserve the valley's virgin beauty for residents and visitors alike.